Teaching
Montessori
in the Home

Teaching Montessori in the Home

by ELIZABETH G. HAINSTOCK

RANDOM HOUSE · NEW YORK

". . . . what you can teach the child and how best
you can teach him depends on what he has learned
before, and, how well he has learned it."

*St. Nicholas' Training Centre
for the Montessori Method of Education, Ltd.*

Fourth Printing
Copyright © 1968 by Elizabeth G. Hainstock
*All rights reserved under International and Pan-American Copyright
Conventions. Published in the United States by Random House,
Inc., New York, and simultaneously in Canada by
Random House of Canada Limited, Toronto.*

Library of Congress Catalog Card Number: 68–14505
*Manufactured in the United States of America
Illustrations by Lee Ames*

CONTENTS

PART III—EARLY SENSORIAL EXERCISES

PART IV—READING AND WRITING EXERCISES

PART V—ARITHMETIC EXERCISES

PART VI—HOME MONTESSORI EQUIPMENT

APPENDIX

For
Katie, Jennifer and Sarah

Teaching Dr. Montessori in the Home

Part 1
Montessori in the Home

An Introduction to Teaching Montessori in the Home

The pressures and fast pace of today's society have taken away the times of quiet togetherness which we should have with our children. It is important to a child's future not to be deprived of this close relationship, and it should be important to you as a mother to have an opportunity to spend time with your young child. We all know how quickly they grow up and leave us, so let us not wait until it is too late.

The opportunity of teaching your child is a thrilling and challenging experience. It enables you to see his progressive steps in learning and to watch him develop into a responsible thinking human being. I feel that it is a unique opportunity, rewarding beyond measure. It nurtures a wonderful closeness between mother and child and will develop a real rapport between you.

It is necessary and important for the parent to fully understand Montessori before attempting to teach it to the child. For this reason, I have included a book list that I feel will be of help to you for background and reference. Teaching Montessori in the home is something that should not be attempted unless you feel that you will be able to carry it through. Your attitude toward your child during this period will have a great effect on him. What the child learns will depend solely on you as his teacher. He possesses the capabilities, but you must arouse them. You as a parent should be able to instinctively sense your child's needs and be able to determine the rate at which you should progress. Always take your lead from the child.

In your zeal to see him progress, you must be careful not to introduce exercises which are too advanced for him. Remember, this is *not* a contest. You are not doing this to impress friends and relatives with little Johnny's remarkable skills, but rather to help give your child a better foundation on which to base his future learning.

The exercises given in this book cover the preschool years from two to five years. I have not attempted to go beyond this stage, as I feel that a child of five should be in a normal school environment with children of his own age. I feel strongly, however, that the child from two to five can be taught effectively and well in the home environment and, in fact, can learn, in many cases, more than he would in school during these formative and sensitive years.

For mothers who are sincerely interested in introducing the Montessori method to their children but, for one reason or another, are not able to send them to a Montessori school, this book, I feel, holds the solution. You do not have to be a teacher to teach Montessori in your home, nor is it necessary to have unlimited space. For the past five years I have had "school" in a small bedroom, shared by my two eldest daughters, and have felt it to be quite satisfactory. After several years of working with Montessori in my own home I am deeply gratified with the results. The older girls learned easily and with enthusiasm, and the younger child, while having been instructed in the simpler exercises, has picked up a considerable amount of more advanced work by imitation and osmosis.

It will not always be possible to have school every day, so teach well when you have the opportunity. However, if a specific time is set aside each day (the morning, after the main household chores have been done, seems to work out best), you will find that "school" becomes a natural part of your daily routine. Your home is first and foremost a home, and this is your only real disadvantage when it comes to turning it into a school. Space is naturally limited, and "school" is a daily temporary situation, unless you are lucky enough to have a spare room used solely for this purpose.

In the beginning you will find that your child is, by nature, more adept at doing some things than others. At first it may seem to you that the child will *never* "catch on," but don't be discouraged. For example, the first few times my eldest child tried to lace a shoe it seemed to me as if she would *never* learn, yet just as I was ready to despair she suddenly began doing it with ease. After several successful lacings she beamed proudly and said, "See, I'm learning!" It is moments like these that make it all worthwhile, and these moments are gratifyingly frequent.

In teaching Montessori in your home, your goal should be to instill in your child a sense of discovery and awareness, as opposed to mere surface learning. If this is done in the early years, it will remain with the child throughout his school experiences and his life.

Maria Montessori: Her Life and Her Method

Maria Montessori was born in Italy in 1870 at Chiaravalle, a small province of Ancona. Because she possessed, as a young child, a great interest and aptitude for mathematics, her parents moved to Rome so that Maria would have the educational advantages of a large city. Encouraged by her parents to become a teacher, she decided instead to venture into the field of engineering. This proved to be not to her liking, and after a brief attraction to biology she made the decision to study medicine—an almost unheard-of pursuit for a young woman of Maria Montessori's era. In 1896 she became the first woman in Italy to take the degree of Doctor of Medicine.

After her graduation from medical school she interned at the Psychiatric Clinic of the University of Rome, and her work here with the mentally deficient led to many of her future ideas. She felt strongly that mental deficiency was more of a pedagogical problem than a medical one and felt that with special educational treatment these handicapped people could be helped. And, in time, her teachings and her understanding resulted in a marked development in the ability of many mentally inferior children.

The first *Casa dei Bambini,* or "Children's House," was established in the slums of Rome in 1907. A prepared environment was provided for these children, all under five years of age. Dr. Montessori used materials previously used to teach older defective children which were primarily scientific apparatus for testing the accuracy of sensory discriminations.

In 1909, as a result of the great interest in the Casa dei Bambini, Maria Montessori published her *Scientific Pedagogy as Applied to Child Education in the Children's Houses.* This work attracted great interest, and Americans were among the first to respond. However, many of her ideas soon met with disapproval, due largely to the fact that Americans were set in their ways of education and could not accept change easily. Many people felt that such extensive training for future development was not warranted for the child of preschool age. Among these were the conservative Darwinians who were strong believers in "fixed intelligence" and who felt that heredity alone determined a child's development. Freud's theories had also gained notice in the early 1900's and tended to minimize the significance of Montessori's revelation that her educational materials awakened the child's *spontaneous* interest in learning.

Despite setbacks Montessori's work continued, and gradually Montessori movements sprang up in many European countries and in different parts of the world. In 1915 Maria Montessori was enthusiastically welcomed to America. She lectured and gave a course for teachers in California. To acquaint more people with her method, a Montessori class was set up at the San Francisco World Exhibition of 1915. Numerous schools were established in the next few years, but they soon closed as interest waned.

Returning to Europe she lectured in many countries and also spent considerable time in further research; many honors were bestowed upon her for her work. During the war years she established the Montessori movement in India, where it is still flourishing today.

Dr. Montessori died in Holland in 1952 at the age of eighty-one. Upon her death her son Mario became her successor in the direction of the Association Montessori Internationale, with headquarters in Amsterdam.

Maria Montessori believed that education begins at birth and that the first few years of life, being the most formative, are the most important, both physically and mentally. Even the smallest baby must be exposed to people and sounds and cuddled and talked to if he is to develop into a normal happy child. The baby has an active mind, which does not wait passively for adult instruction, and he becomes apathetic when constantly left alone. Through normal and gradual learning processes, behavior patterns are established and the powers of the adult mind are gradually built up. Proper learning methods in the years from birth to six years will largely determine the kind of man the child will become. Because mental development in these early years proceeds at a rapid rate, this is a period that must not be wasted.

Montessori felt that in these early years a child has what she referred to as "sensitive periods," during which time he is particularly receptive to certain stimuli. A particular sensitivity toward something lasts only until a necessary need is fulfilled. These periods are perhaps most easily seen in the stages of walking and talking. If parents are aware of these periods, much can be done to help the child at the right time. Observe the child and watch for each particular sensitive period. Then utilize these periods to help him understand and master his environment. All children develop at a different pace, but the following list will help you in knowing when to watch for particular phases of development.

SENSITIVE PERIODS

birth—3 years	Absorbent mind
	Sensory experiences
1½—3 years	Language development
1½—4 years	Coordination and muscle development
	Interest in small objects
2—4 years	Refinement of movement
	Concern with truth and reality
	Aware of order sequence in time and space
2½—6 years	Sensory refinement
3—6 years	Susceptibility to adult influence
3½—4½ years	Writing
4—4½ years	Tactile sense
4½—5½ years	Reading

One of Montessori's biggest concerns was the need to

better understand the child's abilities and capabilities. Too many adults fail to think of a young child as an intelligent human being, capable of learning. Montessori's "discovery of the child" was a true awakening in the advancement of early education. She spoke of the child's mind as the "absorbent mind" because of its great ability to learn and assimilate effortlessly and unconsciously from the world around him. Because of her belief that the child absorbs learning from the physical environment in which he lives, she created a prepared environment for the underprivileged children with whom she worked. She was quick to point out, however, that "the environment should reveal the child, not mold him."

Education need not be imposed on the child; given a learning environment he will be free to act and to develop himself along the lines of his own inner direction. Thus (Montessori felt that there must be freedom within the prepared environment to develop his physical, mental and spiritual growth. The young child is very hand-minded, and the materials are geared to his need to learn through movement, because it is movement that starts the intellect working. The true Montessori classroom is functionally arranged for the child, enabling him to work, move and develop freely) The room itself and all the furniture in it are proportioned to the child's size; his coat is hung on a low hook, and the materials are arranged on shelves that are easily accessible.

Realizing that the child's aesthetic sense is developed in these early years, Maria Montessori stressed the importance of beauty in the classroom. Montessori materials are always well made and well maintained, and neatly arranged on their shelves. The walls are hung with attractive pictures, and numerous books are available to the child. Everything in the classroom has a specific use, and there is nothing there that the child cannot see and touch, for this is how he learns.

Visitors to the first "Children's Houses" were impressed

by the children's spontaneous love of work and by the quiet, busy atmosphere that dominated the room. The materials used by Dr. Montessori in these classrooms awakened the children's interest in learning, and they were taught a love of learning for learning's sake. Montessori felt that if the child was bored and did not react spontaneously to his work, it was not his fault, but rather the fault of the way the work was presented to him.

Her innovations were based largely on her own clinical observations of both mentally retarded and culturally deprived children. Thus her approach to education was scientific.

Dr. Montessori said, "The thing we should cultivate in our teachers is more the *spirit* than the mechanical skill of the scientist—that is, the *direction* of the *preparation* should be toward the spirit rather than toward the mechanism." She presented the teacher as an observer, always ready to guide and direct, whose purpose was to keep alive the child's enthusiasm for learning, without interfering with the child's efforts to teach himself. "In this way we shall notice that the child has a personality which he is seeking to expand; he has initiative, he chooses his own work, persists in it, changes it according to his inner needs; he does not shirk effort, he rather goes in search of it, and with great joy he faces obstacles within his capacity to overcome." The Montessori teacher was taught a respect for the child and his privacy.

(An atmosphere of freedom and liberty of the child is always evident in the Montessori classroom, for Dr. Montessori felt that "the educated hand is a free hand" and that "discipline must come through liberty.") The environment in the Montessori classroom is designed to exclude distractions and to offer opportunities for constructive work. There is a great continuity in Montessori's teaching, for each step is a preparation for a step that follows, and it is to this pattern that her equipment is adapted. The child is given a free choice of activities, and the materials are designed to correspond with his natural physical and physiological development. The teaching method is divided into three parts: motor education, sensory education and language. Great emphasis is placed on a thorough development of the five senses.

As each child will approach the materials and respond to them differently, the children are allowed to proceed at their own pace and the classes are not graded. Montessori believed that each child has "cycles of activity" that should be allowed to be worked through and completed without interruption. In this way the child truly learns according to his own individual needs and capabilities.

The materials designed to develop the senses are all intended to help the child's mind focus on one particular quality. They give the child knowledge in a systematic way so that the order becomes apparent and the child is helped to *know* what he sees. A "control of error" is apparent in all the materials, enabling the child to readily see and correct his own mistakes.

(The Montessori method develops the *whole* personality of the child. His inner activities are cultivated and protected, and freedom within the framework of organization is taught. Montessori felt that she had made "a contribution to the cause of goodness by removing obstacles which were the source of violence and rebellion.)

In this age, where too little stress is placed on a truly good and sound education for the preschooler, Montessori's deep insight and inspired teaching methods can introduce a new and exciting dimension to education. In preschool education today, too little emphasis is placed on continuity in the learning process, and too much is *done* for the child. Learning to learn is an acquired skill which must be taught when the child is young if he is to become a thinking, intelligent individual in later life. The Montessori method has given us the chance to give our children these early advantages. Let us not allow this opportunity to pass unnoticed. If we do, it is our children who will be the losers.

Many Montessori-oriented parents, seeing the great progress of their children in the Montessori classroom ask, "But what will he do when he must leave the Montessori environment and enter the regular school classroom?" The answer is simple. He will be an independent person, with a strong sense of self, who will be able to improvise and use his creativity in working and learning as a healthy, thinking individual. These traits will remain with him throughout his life. What more could any parent ask?

The Importance of the Early Years

Too often the precious fertile years from birth to six years of age are wasted by parents and teachers who feel that the child is too young to learn. In many cases it is actually *they* who are too lazy to teach. Observe the mountains of information that your three-year-old absorbs from watching television. Can you then truly tell yourself that a child of this age is not ready for learning experiences? Take the time to really *talk* to your young child, and you'll be amazed at his storehouse of knowledge. A child must not be allowed to spend the most formative years of his life sitting like a nonentity in his sandbox. By the age of two he has progressed far beyond the stage for idle play and baby talk. Learning at this age is a necessity that must not be thwarted. A young child's curiosity is insatiable, and he should have unlimited opportunities for observation, movement and exploration—in his home, in his garden. Let him discover himself and the world around him. Encourage him to be active and to follow his natural urges, for this is necessary for the development of his character. Remember that what a child *can* be is determined by the foundation laid in these early years, and his capacities are almost limitless.

The child's character is constructed by activity and work during the period from three to six. If a child is continually interrupted and discouraged in his activities during this time, his character development will reflect this disorganization. During the early stages of a child's development he needs encouragement from adults in order to gain confidence in himself. Be free with your praise. A child who is constantly criticized soon loses interest in attempting new things. He also needs stimulation and a sense of security. A semblance of order and routine is important to the young child at this time, for there is so much busyness and confusion around him that he needs familiar "landmarks" on which he can rely. Once a child's daily life begins to show some organization, a sense of order will become evident in everything he does.

Severity and rigid discipline are not good for the very young child because his personality is just beginning to develop, and he is not fully able to understand. For instance, when the very young child constantly handles and touches everything in sight, he is not being naughty—he is only being curious. This is how he learns. Naughtiness seldom becomes a real problem in the life of a normal happy child, who must, however, be taught normal discipline and self-control. He must finish what he starts, for this is a sign of good character, and if he does not develop good work habits, he will not be well prepared for later life.

Children, as Montessori has shown, have a natural desire to learn and work, along with a strong willingness to please. As any observant parent can see, children would rather *learn* than simply be entertained or amused. They do not think of work as something unpleasant. They are constantly looking for new things to do—things that are harder and more challenging. A child may spend much time at some task which to you seems of little consequence, but to him it is very important. As the child grows older and he naturally becomes capable of more complicated forms of activity, he should be allowed to pursue these to further his development. Learning should be fun and a constant source of interest to the young child, as well as to the adult.

Remember too that the young child learns much from imitating adults and other children. In this way they learn both good and bad habits. The child learns, or fails to learn, respect for things from your attitude toward them. It is all well and good for you to stress neatness to your child, but if he is not living in a neat environment he will find this difficult to understand. Setting a good example by what you do benefits a child far more than a lengthy and meaningless explanation.

Expose your child to as much as possible; the wider his scope, the more he will learn. Take him places with you— let him meet new people, see new things, have new experiences. Children learn gradually and naturally from the people with whom they come into contact.

Parents who are fortunate enough to be bilingual should take advantage of this opportunity and introduce a second language to their child. It has been proved that the younger a child is, the more easily he learns and retains another language.

From an early age children want to be independent, but in this era of continual rushing, parents thwart them by being too eager to do things for them. If you will take the time to teach your child to do things for himself, the rewards will be great for both of you. The words you should hear with joy are "Let me do it myself!" We, as parents, must learn to give our children a chance to be self-reliant and to do it with patience and understanding. If some morning your child should show a particular interest in buttoning his own sweater, this is your perfect opportunity to take the time to show him how it is done. Your cardinal rule should be: Never do for a child what he is capable of doing for himself.

The three- or four-year-old takes great pride in doing things for himself. A child of this age is perfectly capable of dressing himself, picking up his toys, making his own bed (though it obviously won't look quite as neat as if you'd made it), and helping with simple chores around the home. He should be allowed to do these things, for the young child must feel that he, like older members of the family, is contributing in some way and has certain jobs and responsibilities. It is just as degrading to the young child as to an adult to have someone constantly doing everything for him. If you give the matter some thought, there are numerous simple tasks that the young child can do around the house. This can save you time, as well as give the child the satisfaction of feeling helpful and needed. Let your child have the practical training that is so necessary to his physical independence. The child must be *taught* independence, and you, the parent, must resist the temptation to always "help" if you care about his future well-being and development. One of the cruelest and most selfish things a parent can do is to make his child completely dependent on him. Parents too often do this because they want to feel needed; by the time they realize their mistake irrevocable damage has been done. A parent who is able to raise a child well and then let him go is a far better parent than one who raises a dependent, clinging creature who cannot lead a life of his own.

Far too many schools today are also guilty of not allowing our children to think for themselves. Children are too often being forced to submit to an unimaginative curriculum in an environment where the teacher makes all the decisions, while the children suffer under the delusion that they are really learning. What they are getting is shallow, superficial learning that profits neither teacher nor pupil. Today's children need far more stimulation than they are being given. They are learning by rote, responding to stock questions with stock answers; too seldom are they allowed to use their minds imaginatively and creatively. On the few occasions when a child or young adult is suddenly presented with a "thought" question, he is unprepared to cope with it—his thinking processes have become stagnant from disuse. It is a pathetic fact that too many young people today are able to think and talk only in vague generalities and abstractions. Is it the fault of the child that he is ill prepared, or does the fault lie within the structure of our present-day educational sysem and, indeed, with the parents themselves, for placing too much emphasis on dependency? Are we raising a generation of pampered, dependent children, who are slowly being allowed to lose all concept of originality and creativity? The importance of teaching our children how to learn and think for themselves in the earliest, formative years cannot be overstressed. A solid, sound framework must be laid, on which the child's future learning—a never-ending process— can be based. The child prepared in this way will not be satisfied with superficial learning but will want to delve more deeply into whatever he studies on his own. A well-developed mind cannot simply be "shut off" when fed shallowly.

Preparing Your Home School

It is important to have a specific place for your school equipment and a specific room in which to conduct "school." Your child should be able to depend on the permanence of this arrangement and know where each piece of equipment may be found. This is a good time to make use of the adage "A place for everything, and everything in its place." The equipment should be arranged in an orderly and attractive fashion, and the child, when finished, must learn to return each thing to its proper place. In this way he is taught respect for things.

I have found that a three- or four-shelf bookcase is excellent for housing materials. I have put casters on the bottom of mine so that it can be easily rolled into the closet when not in use.

The actual Montessori equipment, and the substitutes we will use, all have a "control of error," enabling the child to teach himself and to see and correct his own mistakes. However, it must not be assumed that because of this the materials will teach automatically. The child must be guided in their proper use, as you will see from the lessons.

When demonstrating materials to the child, remember to use a minimum of words and movements. The young child finds it difficult to follow and assimilate a lengthy explanation. Introduce the new materials gradually, according to the directions given. The child should be allowed to work with the materials only after they have been properly presented to him. Don't spoil the freshness of the subject matter by telling the child too much—let him discover for himself and tell *you*.

Be patient. What seems easy for you is of course not necessarily easy for a three-year-old. Remember that the role of the Montessori teacher is that of an observer. In watching your child make an error while attempting to do something, the mother's first impulse is to interrupt with a well-meant "Here, let me show you." Restrain yourself and let him see for himself. He will.

An atmosphere of quiet should prevail at all times during the school period. By this I do not mean absolute silence but rather an atmosphere conducive to concentration and learning. This is not the time for other children in the family to be causing chaos by playing with the school equipment.

When you are ready to begin, explain to the child that you are going to have school. In the first day introduce two or three things, and let the child work with them. Each succeeding day introduce one or two more things, and allow the child to work also with things presented on preceding days. During the course of the school period the only visible materials should be those which the child is using at that particular time. As he progresses beyond certain materials, they should be removed. Materials that are too advanced should not be in the room. Always take your lead from the child, and proceed according to his interests and capabilities.

The child should be permitted to choose what he wants to work with and to repeat or stop as he pleases. However, each task *must* be completed before the material is returned to its place. He must not be allowed to stop simply because he has lost interest. Perseverance is a good lesson in self-discipline.

In the beginning, the "school" equipment should be used by the child only during school time and with supervision. The child must not be allowed to play with the materials whenever he wishes. Unless he is taught that they are intended for a specific time and purpose, he will lose respect for them as teaching devices. However, you will find that after working at home in this way for several months you will reach the point where the child is familiar with each piece of equipment. Then, and only then, may he be allowed to work at random hours.

The school exercises may be done in the child's own room or in another room set aside for this purpose. Practical-life exercises are probably best done in the kitchen, particularly when water or other potential mess makers are involved. Practical-life exercises may also be done at times other than the actual school time; for example, when you are dusting the house, this is the perfect time to introduce the child to this task.

The time spent with school should be no more than one and a half to two hours, at preferably the same time each day. In the first few weeks, however, or if you are working with a very young child, forty-five minutes are ample. Gradually increase the time spent. You must also try to sense when it is time to stop. Stop while the child is still enjoying what he is doing, rather than waiting until he loses interest and then announcing, "No more school."

If for any reason you or your child simply are not in the mood, it is far better to miss a day than to proceed. School should be a time of togetherness for you and your child—a time to enjoy being with each other and learning together. If it becomes a chore, stop immediately. Nothing will be gained by continuing. Your attitude is all-important during this learning period.

In teaching your child, you must be very careful to avoid boredom. Dr. Montessori felt that if the child became bored the fault lay in the way the materials had been presented to him. Children love repetition, but not when it's overdone. They will lose interest if you progress too slowly, and if you go too quickly the materials will be beyond their comprehension.

All of the equipment used in this book can be made or obtained relatively inexpensively. (A list of educational toys and their specific uses is in the Appendix.) In the following pages I will describe materials and substitutes I have adapted and used successfully in my own home with my three children. I have adapted Montessori equipment and classroom exercises and lessons to make them suitable for home use. Although most of the material closely follows the Montessori school procedure, it is most important in working at home to teach the child to function in his home environment. With a bit of ingenuity you should be able to further adapt certain things to better suit your own particular needs, assuming of course that the end result will be the same. For example, if storage space is limited, hollow blocks which may be nested are preferable to solid blocks which must be stacked and take up considerable space. Common sense and imagination are important to the application of ideas.

Opportunities for practical-life exercises are endless. Remember how much the child learns by imitation. Let him do things which he would normally see done in his natural environment. In this way he is better able to understand the functioning of his own particular environment and becomes more aware of the things around him. What he learns will be up to you!

Prepared Environment for the Home

The Montessori schools have a "prepared environment," where everything is proportioned to the child's size; so too should the home be adjusted to a child's needs. It is an adult world, and we often forget how difficult it is for a child to function adequately in this environment. Things for your child should be scaled to his size and be made easily accessible to him in order to facilitate his learning to work and to help himself.

There are many ingenious ways of "fixing up" your child's room. For example, you can probably find a table, chair and bookcase or cupboard in any second-hand store and alter them to suit your needs. Or buy what is called a sink cut-out from any hardware or lumber dealer and to this attach four 18-inch legs. You will then have a formica-topped table just the right size for your child. For practical-life training the Bissell Little Queen set is ideal—it contains an apron, carpet sweeper, mop, broom, sponge and dustpan. It may be found at any toy shop or obtained with trading stamps.

In setting up your home school your "prepared environment" should include:

A table and chair proportionate to the child's size, and lightweight so that he may carry them with ease

A cupboard or shelves low enough to enable the child to reach all parts of it

A piece of oilcloth (the size of the table top) to be used when working with things that might spill or mark the table

Child-size cleaning equipment for practical-life exercises

Low hooks for clothes

Low drawers for frequently used clothing

Part II
Practical-Life Exercises

The Practical Situation

The exercises for practical life are designed to teach the child to function in his own environment by teaching him how to cope with the things around him. The daily functions of our home are routine and simple to us, but they are new and exciting to a child. He must learn that there is a correct way of doing whatever needs to be done in the home. So often we will scold a young child for banging drawers shut and yet have we ever taken the time to show him the proper way of opening and closing drawers? It is only after he has learned to master his home environment that the child is ready to begin the more complicated processes of learning.

Let the child observe the tasks involved in the care of his home, and let him see that it must be kept orderly and clean. Let him observe you as you do chores around the house, and allow him to help you. Young children love to imitate adults and think that arranging flowers, making beds and cleaning house are fun.

Children love to work with their hands—an important activity in their development. Teach the child to be responsible for his own room and personal belongings, and let him have simple chores that are strictly his to do (such as emptying the wastebaskets, cleaning his room and putting away groceries). Let him know that he does these chores because they are his responsibility, not because he may expect a reward from you.

Let us utilize the tremendous amounts of energy our children possess!

OPENING AND CLOSING DRAWERS
AGE 2½–4

MATERIALS: The child's own chest of drawers

DEMONSTRATION:
1) Place the first two fingers and thumb on each knob or handle.
2) Open and close one drawer noiselessly and carefully.
3) Proceed in this manner with the remaining drawers, then have the child do it.

PURPOSE: To teach the child an appreciation of quiet and order
To give the child a sense of achievement when he opens and closes the drawers quietly

CONTROL OF ERROR: Drawers should make no noise.

BUSY BOARD OR
DRESSING FRAMES
AGE 2½–5

MATERIALS: The busy board or the individual dressing frames (Instructions for making busy board on page 90, for dressing frames on page 91)

DEMONSTRATION:
1) Present the frame to the child in its complete state.
2) Take the two sides apart, slowly and deliberately, and then reassemble it in the same way.
3) Let the child count the buttons, feel the fabrics, etc. Tell him the names of the things involved and what they are used for.

PURPOSE: To teach self-reliance, self-control and coordination of movements.

CONTROL OF ERROR: The child is able to see if it has been improperly done.

POURING RICE
AGE 2½–5

MATERIALS: Oilcloth for table top

Small tray bearing a small glass and a small pitcher (or a 1-cup plastic measuring cup) which is half filled with rice

DEMONSTRATION:

1) Point to the various objects and name them for the child ("glass," "pitcher," "handle," "spout," etc.).

2) Grasp the pitcher handle with the first two fingers and thumb.

3) Grasp the glass with the other hand.

4) Place the lip of the pitcher opposite the rim of the glass and exactly over its center.

5) Pour from the pitcher to the glass.

6) Repeat until the exercise is perfectly performed.

PURPOSE: To develop the muscles involved in pouring

To teach the child to pour from pitcher to cup in a neat fashion

To teach self-reliance

CONTROL OF ERROR: Errors cause spills.

NOTE:

When the pouring of rice is perfected, you may advance to water and then to letting the child pour his own milk and juice, etc. You will also find that much time and energy can be saved if you teach the child to use a sponge to clean up anything he spills.

DUSTING
AGE 2½–5

MATERIALS: A duster, a wastebasket, a dusty table

DEMONSTRATION:
1) Notice dust on the table.
2) Brush away from the body with the duster, working from the near to the far side.
3) Dust the table legs and sides, as well as the top.
4) Pick up anything that interferes with the dusting, and dust under these things, not around them.
5) Put everything back in order.
6) Shake duster into basket.

PURPOSE: To learn that dust, which gathers daily, must be eliminated

To learn neatness and responsibility of keeping things neat and clean

CONTROL OF ERROR: If not properly done, some dust will remain.

CARRYING A CHAIR
AGE 2½–5

MATERIAL:	Child's chair
DEMONSTRATION:	1) Grasp the back of the chair with one hand and the front of the seat with the other hand, stooping over as you do this.
	2) Movements should be deliberate and as noiseless as possible.
	3) Straighten, and standing erect carry the chair to a specified place, avoiding other persons and objects.
	4) Chair seat should be kept level at all times.
	5) Lower chair carefully into position so that no noise is heard.
PURPOSE:	To teach coordination, independence and concentration. To develop precision and care of handling objects, and to do this quietly
CONTROL OF ERROR:	While carrying the chair the child can hear any noise or feel any bumps.

FOLDING A NAPKIN
AGE 2½–5

MATERIAL: Square napkin or piece of cloth

(This can be marked or stitched to show the child where to make folds)

DEMONSTRATION:
1) Lay napkin flat on table.
2) Bring sides together.
3) To make an oblong, fold once again. To make a triangle, place diagonal corners together.
4) Flatten crease with hand.
5) As you make the folds, mention to the child the names of the shapes you are forming: "This is a square," "This is a triangle," etc.

PURPOSE: To develop muscular control of fingers, which is training in precision

To teach child to help in his own environment

CONTROL OF ERROR: An improperly folded napkin will appear sloppy.

SETTING A TABLE
AGE 2½–5

MATERIALS: Table, silverware, place mats, napkins

DEMONSTRATION:
1) Place mats on table.
2) Arrange silverware, explaining where each piece goes.
3) The first few times, work with just the knife and fork.
4) Then add the spoon and napkin.
5) Add other things as child becomes adept at the basic setting (e.g., salt and pepper, plates, cups, flowers, etc.)

PURPOSE: To develop control of movement and coordination

To teach appreciation of manners and social amenities

CONTROL OF ERROR: A properly set table will look attractive and correct.

NOTE: At first, use the child's table and his play implements; then allow him to set the family table.

WASHING DISHES
AGE 2½–5

MATERIALS:

Sink, sponge, dishes, dish drainer, apron, soap, towel

DEMONSTRATION:

1) Invite child to watch you.
2) Put on apron.
3) Partially fill one sink with water for washing, and the other with rinse water. (If you have a single sink, place the rinse water in a plastic sink.)
4) Pour soap into the wash water.
5) Place a dish in the water.
6) Wash it with sponge and place it in rinse water.
7) Rinse and place in drainer.
8) Proceed in this manner until all dishes are washed, rinsed and set in drainer.
9) Drain water from sinks and clean them.
10) Wring out sponge and return sponge and soap to their places.
11) Dry dishes with towel, showing child how to hold the towel and dish properly.
12) As each dish is dried, place it on drainboard.

13) When all dishes are dried, put them away in their proper places.

14) Remove apron and put apron and towel away.

PURPOSE: To teach muscle coordination and to give the child a sense of enjoyment and achievement in doing household chores

CONTROL OF ERROR: Spilled water, broken dishes or soiled dishes

WASHING HANDS
AGE 3–4

MATERIALS: Bathroom or kitchen sink, soap, nailbrush, towel, hand lotion

DEMONSTRATION:
1) Let child stand on chair at sink and roll up sleeves.
2) Place drain in sink and partially fill with tepid water.
3) Place hands in water.
4) Rub soap on hands, then return it to its place.
5) Rub each soapy palm over back of hands and rub each finger from tip to base—use nailbrush if necessary.
6) Rinse soap off in water.
7) Drain water from sink.
8) With towel, dry each finger, then rest of hand.
9) Hang towel on rack.
10) Use small amount of hand lotion, rubbing into hands with circular motion.

PURPOSE: To learn control of movement and to complete a cycle of activity

To teach care of self and self-reliance

CONTROL OF ERROR: Examination of hands reveals if properly washed.

WASHING A TABLE
AGE 3–4

MATERIALS: Child's table, pitcher of water, two small pails or bowls (one for rinsing, one for washing), sponge, drying cloth

DEMONSTRATION:
1) Cover the floor underneath the table with a large cloth or paper.
2) Pour water from the pitcher into each pail, adding soap to one.
3) Dip sponge in soap water, wring partially dry.
4) With soapy sponge, scrub table top, working from outer edges to the center.
5) Remove any lingering spots.
6) Rinse sponge well.
7) Dip sponge into rinse water, squeeze until partially dry, then wipe table top until soap is removed.
8) With drying cloth, carefully wipe table until thoroughly dry.
10) Empty water from basins and return all materials to their proper places.

PURPOSE: To teach care of environment, sequence of action and control of movement

CONTROL OF ERROR: Table should be clean with no traces of soap or dirt.

SWEEPING THE FLOOR
AGE 3–5

MATERIALS: Broom, dustpan, wastebasket

DEMONSTRATION:

1) Call attention to debris on floor and speak of desirability of neatness.

2) Hold broom correctly and easily, sweeping from far sides to center and moving furniture when necessary.

3) Brush gathered debris into small pile in center of floor.

4) Holding dustpan in left hand, and broom in right, lean over and brush debris into dustpan.

5) Empty contents of dustpan into wastebasket.

6) Put furniture and sweeping implements back in their proper places.

PURPOSE: To teach cleanliness and care of environment

CONTROL OF ERROR: If not properly done, the floor will not be clean.

POLISHING SILVER
AGE 3–5

MATERIALS: Apron, silver polish, silverware, oiling cloth, polishing cloth

DEMONSTRATION:
1) Apply polish to cloth.
2) Apply polish to tarnished silverware, rubbing until cloth is free of polish.
3) Replace cap on polish.
4) Return polish and cloth to their proper places.
5) Rinse silverware, dry thoroughly.
6) Return silverware to its proper place.

PURPOSE: To show the satisfaction of seeing perfection emerge from imperfection through one's own efforts

To teach the care of the child's own environment and possessions

CONTROL OF ERROR: Cleanliness of silverware

SHINING SHOES
AGE 3–5

MATERIALS: Newspaper, pair of shoes, shoe polish, brush and cloth

DEMONSTRATION:
1) Place newspaper on floor.
2) Remove dirt from shoes with brush.
3) Hold shoe in place with left hand and with right hand cover shoe with polish, which has been placed on cloth.
4) Repeat process on second shoe.
5) Let shoes dry while you replace lid on polish.
6) Shine shoes with cloth.
7) When job is completed, return things to their proper places.

PURPOSE: To teach the care of personal possessions and to teach the completion of a work cycle
To develop coordination and dexterity

CONTROL OF ERROR: Any errors or sloppiness will be readily seen.

LACING A SHOE
AGE 3½–5

MATERIAL: Wooden lacing boot or busy board

DEMONSTRATION:
1) Place shoe on table in front of child.
2) Slowly unlace shoe.
3) Relace shoe, using exaggerated motions so that the child can see how the laces cross each other and go through consecutive holes.
4) Simply lace the shoe at this point—don't bother about tying the bow.

PURPOSE: To teach the child independence in dressing himself
To develop hand-eye coordination and muscular control

CONTROL OF ERROR: If improperly laced, the shoe will appear sloppy.

TYING A BOW
AGE 4–5

MATERIAL: Lacing boot or busy board

DEMONSTRATION:

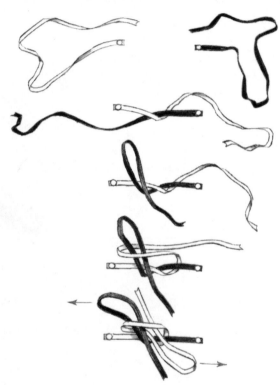

1) Place the laces on the table in front of the child. (If you use two contrasting colors of twill tape it will be easier for the child to see and understand what is being done.)
2) The first day, simply let the child tie the first half knot.
3) The second day, show him how to make a loop with one piece, then bring the second piece around the loop and through it.
4) The third step is to demonstrate how to grasp one loop in the right hand and one in the left, then pull until your bow is made and secured.
5) Proceed slowly with bow tying, making sure that the child is fully understanding the various steps.

PURPOSE: To develop muscle control
To learn completion of a cycle
To teach independence in dressing oneself

CONTROL OF ERROR: An improperly tied bow will appear sloppy.

Finger-Dexterity Exercises
BEAD STRINGING
AGE 1½–4

MATERIALS: Multicolored beads for string-ing

Lace or string knotted at one end (or use empty thread spools and shoelace)

DEMONSTRATION:
1) Show child how to string beads.
2) Depending upon the age and ability of the child, the following exercises may be introduced:
    a) Group all the like colors together.
    b) String one of each color in consecutive pattern.
    c) String two of one color, three of an-other, etc.
    d) Proceed in this man-ner, using your own ideas, and the child's.

BOTTLES AND TOPS
AGE 2–4

MATERIALS: Four to six bottles or jars of differing sizes, with tops (keep these in a small box or container)

DEMONSTRATION:
1) Place bottles on table in front of child.
2) Slowly and silently unscrew tops, then replace them.
3) First do them in order, then mix tops and let child do the same.

USING A DROPPER
AGE 2½–5

MATERIALS: Bottle with dropper, filled half full of water

Small bottle or container on tray

DEMONSTRATION:
1) Place tray on table.
2) Unscrew top of bottle with dropper.
3) With thumb and index finger pinch dropper so that water is drawn into it.
4) Unpinch and bring hand to empty container. Holding dropper, again pinch top so that water is expelled into bottle.
5) Repeat this process until water is transferred from dropper bottle into empty bottle. Transfer water back and forth between bottles in this manner.

CUTTING
AGE 3–5

MATERIALS:

Blunt-end scissors
Paper
Wastebasket

DEMONSTRATION:

1) Show child the proper way to hold scissors and manipulate them.
2) Hold scissors with one hand and paper with other.
3) Show how to cut the narrowest strips possible from the outside edges of the paper.
4) Teach child to cut over wastebasket or other receptacle, to avoid mess.

Painting and Coloring

Allow the child as much freedom as possible in painting and coloring. Make drawing materials easily accessible to him as soon as he is old enough (usually around three years) to understand their proper use. Give him large sheets of paper, such as butcher paper or large rolls of newsprint, which are always fun for the beginner to work on and are easily obtainable. Washable crayons are recommended. Powdered tempera paints are convenient, as they are easily stored and can be mixed in small quantities. Finger painting too is a real delight for the preschooler. Easels may be purchased or easily made, and are conveniently stored when not in use.

Let the child decide what he wants to draw, and then tell you about it. Don't thwart his spontaneity and self-expression by demanding that he draw specific things. And, above all, never criticize your child's attempts at art. Accept his definition of what he has drawn—if he says it's a cat, then it's a cat, regardless of what it may look like to you!

Drawing Fun for the Three- to Five-Year-Old

Trace the child's outline on a large piece of paper, and let him fill in his features, clothing, etc.

Draw various shapes for the child to color, and tell him to keep within the lines.

Allow the child to trace pictures in coloring books or magazines. This is good eye-hand control and helps his accuracy, which is later so important to writing.

Let him be free to draw what he wants.

Working with Clay

Clay is a marvelous implement of self-expression for the young child. As with drawing, let him choose his own subject matter. The younger child enjoys rolling clay out with a rolling pin, then making shapes with cookie cutters. Eventually he will begin making three-dimensional figures. The feel of clay and the joy of creating with it are a real thrill for the preschooler as well as for the older child.

Doing Puzzles

Puzzles are particularly good for the child's eye-hand coordination and dexterity. Begin with the simple ones and gradually work up to those that are more difficult. The puzzles with knobs on the pieces are excellent because they teach the child to grasp objects such as pencils. If the pieces lack knobs, this can be easily remedied by sticking an upholstery tack in the center of each piece. For the child of a year and a half to two, puzzles consisting of a few large easy-to-handle pieces are best. Puzzles with all animals, flowers, transportation vehicles and so forth are good learning devices for the three- to four-year-old, while the older more adept child can progress to more complicated figure and scene puzzles. Demonstrate the puzzle to the child with slow and deliberate motions, then let him try to figure it out for himself. Do not give him too much help beyond the initial introduction.

The child of four can work with his movable alphabet and puzzles. For example, if the puzzle is one of figures or animals, write the name of the object underneath its shape. Let the child remove each puzzle piece, one at a time, and set it on the floor. By looking at its name, with the movable alphabet he will be able to spell it out by simply matching the letters.

Sewing

The child of four or five loves to sew and this is a marvelous exercise for the fingers and eye-hand control. Cardboard sewing cards, purchased at any toy shop, may be used at first. Then outline figures can be drawn on burlap or any loose-weave fabric, and using wool or cotton thread, the child can use a running stitch to sew along the outline. Sewing large buttons on fabric is another exercise children delight in, and when greater proficiency is achieved they can begin to sew buttons on their own clothes. Be sure to instruct them in the proper way to thread a needle and knot the thread at the end. A thimble too comes in handy. The older children can progress to making simple things such as glasses cases or small purses and eventually to working on stitchery kits sold in local stores.

Nature Study

Young children have an innate interest in nature and a great curiosity for learning more about the things around them. Nature study is an area that should not be neglected in the preschooler's education. Follow the child's natural interest and inclinations, and when he shows interest in a particular facet of nature, take the time to explain it more fully to him. There are numerous things you can do to increase your child's knowledge of nature. Here are a few suggestions for home nature study:

Show the child how to plant bulbs or seeds, either in the yard or in pots. Teach him to care for them properly, and explain their growth and development.

Teach the child the different parts of a flower (stem, leaf, petals, stamen, pistils, etc.), of a tree (trunk, roots, limbs, leaves, etc.), and of leaves. Make him aware of the different sizes and shapes of flowers, trees and leaves.

Help your child to plant a small vegetable garden and care for it. The young child takes great pride in seeing something from *his* garden on the dinner table.

Show the child the proper way to cut flowers and arrange them in a vase. He can also be of great help if he learns to trim back dead flowers.

Tell him about the various insects found in his yard—what they do, the parts of their body, how they live in the yard.

Let him do indoor gardening, such as "planting" an avocado pit in water and watching it root.

Allow your child to have some kind of animal to care for, whether it be a fish or a turtle or a larger animal. Explain the different parts of an animal to him (paws, whiskers, muzzle, shell, etc.).

Look in stores and libraries for books on nature and animals, and watch the magazines for pictures you can use in teaching your child.

Collect pictures of zoo animals, farm animals, jungle animals and such, and teach the child more about them and how they live.

Collect individual pictures of mother animals and their babies. Mount them on pieces of cardboard and let the child match the mothers to the babies.

Most stores have "flash cards" for mammals, insects and the like which can be both great fun and educational.

Geography

Geography is another fascinating subject for children. As the child becomes familiar with his own environment he becomes interested in other people and their environment. Again, take your lead from the child and his interests and activities. For example, if he has a new friend from another state, take the time to point the state out to him on the map and tell him something about it. Buy him a map puzzle of the United States and a paper map or globe of the world. Tell him what parts of the country produce various farm crops and where various things we own come from. Cut out magazine pictures of children of other lands and discuss their life and culture. Young children particularly enjoy hearing about the clothing and homes of people from other countries. Let him take books from the library dealing with the subject and help him to develop an interest in the world around him.

Part III
Early Sensorial Exercises

The Sensorial Situation

Sensorial exercises are concerned with the development and refinement of the five senses, thereby sharpening the child's intellect and control and preparing him for the more advanced exercises. The child learns by using both his hands and his mind; this principle has been followed in developing the sensorial materials described below.

At first glance many of these exercises may seem very simple to you, as indeed they are. But try to think of them from a young child's point of view—to him they are all new and difficult.

Before introducing the various lessons, be sure to note the age for which they are intended. This is important. The two- and a half-year-old is not able to do work intended for a four-year-old, nor should the four-year-old have to do work at the two- or three-year level if he has advanced beyond that. Remember that each step leads to another, and you must proceed in an orderly and progressive pattern. It is for this reason that the exercises in this book have been placed in a specific order.

The Three-Period Lesson

The purpose of the three-period lesson is to help the child to better understand the materials and to allow you to see how well the child is grasping and absorbing what you are showing him. The three-period lesson should be used with every demonstration. It is also helpful in enlarging the child's vocabulary. When working with the materials, show him the different objects and compare. For example:

large—small   large—larger—largest
rough—smooth   small—smaller—smallest
light—heavy   big—little
hard—soft

In presenting the lessons for the education of the senses, the order should be:

First Period: *Recognition of identity*
Make the association between the object being shown and its name. "This is——." Repeat until you feel that the child understands the association.

Second Period: *Recognition of contrasts*
To assure that the child understands, say "Give me the——."

Third Period: *Discrimination between similar objects*

See if the child remembers the name himself. Point to the various objects, saying "Which one is this?" He should be able to say the name correctly. If not, help him. Repeat until he is able to do it.

THE TOWER
AGE 2½–4

MATERIALS: Building blocks of gradated size

DEMONSTRATION:

1) Place the blocks on table or rug.
2) Select the largest cube and place it in front of the child.
3) With careful and deliberate movements continue in this manner until all blocks have been built up in tower-like fashion, from largest to smallest.
4) Count the number of blocks.
5) Name the colors (if they differ).
6) Blow the blocks from the tower, explaining that the light ones fall, while the heavy ones remain in place.
7) Use the three-period lesson.

PURPOSE: To develop coordination of movement and visual and tactile perception of dimensions

CONTROL OF ERROR: If the tower is not correctly built, it will topple. If blocks are not placed in gradated order, blocks will not fit correctly.

CYLINDERS AND SOLID INSETS
AGE 2½–5

MATERIALS:

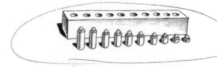

Four blocks, each containing ten wooden cylinders in ten holes. Each cylinder has a round knob for easy grasping. The cylinders in the blocks vary in the following manner:

Block A: same height, diameter of different widths

Block B: same diameter, length decreases

Block C: diameter decreases, length decreases

Block D: diameter increases, length decreases

DEMONSTRATION:

1) Place block on table.
2) Remove cylinders very carefully.
3) Replace first in order, then mixed.
4) Repeat procedure with Blocks B, C, and D.
5) Use positions as shown below.

Two: Three: Four:

6) Later do exercise with blindfold.

PURPOSE:

Visual and tactile education of differing dimensions

Preparation for holding pencils, etc.

Muscular coordination for hands and arm

CONTROL OF ERROR: There will be no cylinder left when replaced properly.

Having these cylinders is optional, but they are excellent learning devices. They may be purchased from Creative Playthings.

FABRIC BASKET
AGE 2½–5

MATERIALS: A small basket or box containing two each of a variety of differently textured fabrics cut into squares (e.g., silk, cotton, terry cloth, corduroy, mohair)

DEMONSTRATION:
1) Present to the child three pairs of fabrics with the greatest contrast in texture.
2) Mix them and ask him to pair them by feeling them between his fingers.
3) When he understands the procedure, add more fabrics.
4) Encourage him to match them blindfolded or with his eyes closed.

PURPOSE: To develop and refine the tactile sense

CONTROL OF ERROR: If an error is made, the last pair won't match.

THERMAL BOTTLES
AGE 2½–4

MATERIALS: Thermal bottles (Instructions for preparing bottles on page 94)

DEMONSTRATION:
1) Touch each container noiselessly and deliberately.
2) Explain "This is cold," "This is hot," "This is colder than——," etc.
3) Proceed in this manner with each container, letting the child feel with his own fingers.

PURPOSE: To develop tactile sense
To identify similar and dissimilar temperatures, and to distinguish between them

CONTROL OF ERROR: Inability to differentiate and describe the temperature

BUTTON GAMES, PART 1
AGE 2½–3

MATERIALS:	Six buttons in each of three or four contrasting colors
	A dish or container for each of the colors
DEMONSTRATION:	1) Show the child how to place all the buttons of one color in individual dishes.
	2) Add more buttons of different colors, if you wish.
	3) Teach the child the names of the colors; count the buttons.
	4) Use the three-period lesson.
PURPOSE:	To teach the child to differentiate between colors
CONTROL OF ERROR:	The child can see if buttons have been misplaced.

BUTTON GAMES, PART 2
AGE 3–5

MATERIALS: Twenty-four buttons of the same color and type, consisting of six buttons in each of four closely gradated sizes and containers for each size

DEMONSTRATION:
1) Show child how to put all of the buttons of one size into a container.
2) Blindfold him and let him divide the buttons by feel.

PURPOSE: To teach the child to differentiate between similar sizes and shapes

CONTROL OF ERROR: The child is able to see if buttons have been misplaced.
Muffin tins are excellent for sorting.

ROUGH AND SMOOTH BOARDS
AGE 2½–4

MATERIALS: Three wooden rectangular boards, made from instructions for making rough and smooth boards, page 92.

DEMONSTRATION:
1) Show the child how to feel the first board, lightly from top to bottom—first one half, then the other.
2) Explain: "This is smooth," "This is rough."
3) Add the second and the third boards gradually when the child seems ready, using the same procedure.
4) When the child understands the exercise, encourage him to do it blindfolded or with his eyes closed.

PURPOSE: To refine the tactile sense
To develop awareness of textures
To develop the light touch necessary to writing

CONTROL OF ERROR: Inability to distinguish differences in textures

SILENCE GAME
AGE 2½–5

MATERIALS: Household noises and noises of human movement around us

DEMONSTRATION:
1) Ask your child to sit quietly next to you.
2) Explain to him that he makes silence by being very still and not moving.
3) Ask him to be very quiet and to listen to how many sounds he can hear. Ask him to see how quietly he can breathe, sit, etc.
4) Ask him to go to the other end of the room quietly and to return quietly when he hears you whisper his name.
5) Discuss with him various quiet sounds (breathing, rustling of leaves, household noises, etc.).

PURPOSE: To fulfill an inner need in the child and to develop ability to concentrate

CONTROL OF ERROR: The child will notice his own noises.

WALKING THE LINE
AGE 3–5

MATERIAL: A six-foot piece of string or yarn

DEMONSTRATION:
1) Stretch the string into a straight line on the floor.
2) Show the child how to walk on the line, one foot in front of the other; stress good balance.
3) Let the child walk on the line carrying various objects and as quietly as he can.
4) Place the string in different shapes—circle, ellipse, figure eight, letter of child's name, etc., and proceed as above.

PURPOSE: To stress good balance, posture, and graceful movement

CONTROL OF ERROR: The child walking off the line or making noise while carrying objects

BARIC TABLETS
AGE 3–5

MATERIALS: Five or six baric tablets (Instructions for making baric tablets on page 91)

DEMONSTRATION:
1) Let the child hold each tablet in his hand, one at a time.
2) Find the heaviest, then the next heaviest, and so on.
3) Place the tablets on the table in order, from heaviest to lightest.
4) Let the child do this blindfolded, after he has become familiar with the exercise.

PURPOSE: To develop the child's sense of weight

CONTROL OF ERROR: The tablets will be incorrectly placed.

MYSTERY BAG
AGE 3–5

MATERIALS: A bag filled with eight to ten familiar objects (e.g., comb, whistle, shoelace)

DEMONSTRATION:
1) Blindfold the child, or have him close his eyes.
2) Let him reach into the bag and withdraw one object.
3) Have him identify the object by feeling its parts.
4) Each time this exercise is done, the objects in the bag may be changed, and depending on the child's age, simple or difficult objects may be used.
5) This exercise may also be done with objects having names beginning with specific alphabet letters. For example, if the child is working with *s* you might place such things as ship, sock, spoon in the bag.

PURPOSE: To develop familiarity with various objects
To develop tactile sense

CONTROL OF ERROR: A mistake in identification

SOUND BOTTLES
AGE 3–5

MATERIALS:	Six pairs of bottles (Instructions for making sound bottles on page 93)
DEMONSTRATION:	1) Remove bottles from the box and place on the table.
	2) Take one bottle and shake it.
	3) Using bottles with contrasting tops, shake until a matching sound is found.
	4) Pair all bottles by this method.
	5) When the child has learned this exercise, let him pair the bottles and grade them as loud, medium, or soft.
PURPOSE:	To develop sensitivity of the auditory sense
CONTROL OF ERROR:	If an error is made, the last pair won't match.

COLOR TABLETS
AGE 3–5

MATERIALS: Tablets (Instructions for making color tablets on page 94)

DEMONSTRATION:
1) Take Box I to the table.
2) Take the colors out of the box and mix them on the table in front of the child.
3) Pick up one of the tablets and show it to the child, asking "Can you find me another one like this?" When he does, place the tablets together and repeat this process with the others.
4) Use the three-period lesson, and also tell him the color names.
5) When the child is able to do the exercise, present Box II in the same way.
6) From Box III take a set of boards and show the child how to arrange them in gradation, going from darkest to lightest.

PURPOSE: To develop color appreciation and sensitivity to the harmony of color

CONTROL OF ERROR: There must be visual harmony in the gradation of color.

SCENT BOTTLES
AGE 3–5

MATERIALS: Six pairs of bottles, containing dry spices (Instructions for preparing scent bottles on page 93)

DEMONSTRATION:
1) Take the bottles to the child's table and remove the tops.
2) Smell the bottles and show the child how to pair them by smell; replace the bottle tops.

PURPOSE: To develop the child's olfactory sense

To make him aware of different and like smells

CONTROL OF ERROR: The last pair won't smell the same.

GEOMETRIC INSETS, PART 1
AGE 2½–5

MATERIALS: Six geometric shapes in frames (Instructions for making geometric insets, page 108)

DEMONSTRATION:

1) Using one shape at a time, take inset and frame to the child's table and remove inset from frame.
2) Going clockwise, trace with the index finger the outside of the inset and the outline of the frame's inside edge.
3) Tell the child, "This is a circle," etc.
4) Ask the child to point out objects in the room that are circles.
5) Proceed in this manner with the remaining geometric shapes, using Steps 1 to 4 for each, as well as using the three-period lesson.
6) Show the child how each inset fits into its own frame.
7) Finally present the full tray of insets and frames, remove all insets, and have child replace them.

PURPOSE: To learn differences in shapes

CONTROL OF ERROR: Insets will fit only in their correct frame.

GEOMETRIC INSETS, PART 2
AGE 3–5

MATERIALS:
Six geometric insets
Two colored pencils
Pieces of paper cut the same size as frames

DEMONSTRATION:
1) Place the frame (without the inset) evenly on a piece of paper.
2) With pencil, trace around the inner edge of the frame.
3) Remove the frame and draw lines across the shape, going from left to right and staying within the lines.
4) When Step 3 is done with ease, repeat Steps 1 and 2, and then
5) Show the child how to place a corresponding inset directly over the drawing and trace around this with a pencil of contrasting color.
6) Later, show the child how he can use more than one inset and make various patterns.

PURPOSE:
To prepare the child's hand for writing
To develop good eye-hand coordination and control

CONTROL OF ERROR:
The child can see if he has not stayed within the lines.

NOTE: When the child's eye-hand coordination appears to be good,
let him begin to write. Start
with simple words and his
name.

GEOMETRIC SHAPES
AGE 3½–5

MATERIALS: Cards with geometric shapes in
six to eight gradated sizes (Use
triangle, square, circle, etc.)

DEMONSTRATION: 1) Take the six triangle cards
and spread them on the
table.

2) Tell the child the name of
the shape.

3) Ask him to find the largest
triangle and place it at the
top corner of his table.

4) Find the next largest and
place it under the largest.
Proceed in this manner until all six triangles are laid
out in gradation, from largest to smallest.

5) Continue in the same way
with the outer shapes.

PURPOSE: To learn geometric forms and
to become aware of gradations

CONTROL OF ERROR: The child will see his mistake
if the proper size is incorrectly
placed.

NAMING THE COLORS
AGE 4½–5

MATERIALS:	Color circles (Instructions for making color circles on page 95)
DEMONSTRATION:	1) Present the circles one at a time to the child.
	2) Point to the written name and say "Red," or whatever.
	3) Go through this procedure with each color circle, letting the child repeat after you the name of the color.
	4) Let the child go through the circles and tell you the colors.
PURPOSE:	To enable the child to associate the name with the color it represents.

Part IV
Reading and Writing Exercises

Language Development

Reading and writing go hand in hand, and the early work with the Montessori sensorial materials prepares the child for the introduction to both. Montessori observed that young children often have "an explosion into writing," and because of their early sensorial experiences, writing usually comes before actual reading.

Through the sensorial exercises the child has learned the delicate handling of all the materials and has refined his movement of hand and fingers by using such materials as the cylinders and knobbed puzzles. These exercises are preparatory to handling the pencil. His sensitivity of touch has developed through the tactile exercises (rough and smooth boards, fabric basket, etc.), and the eye has been trained through the sensorial exercises for developing eye-hand coordination. This indirect preparation for writing is achieved by the development and refinement of the senses of touch, sight and sound.

The child must have mastery of the pencil before he is able to begin forming letters, and he is helped in acquiring this skill by the geometric-insets exercise. This also enables the child to perfect his eye-hand coordination and control, without which good writing is not possible. When he has become adept at working with the insets and has achieved good pencil control, he is then able to begin writing actual letters and, soon after, words.

Through the use of the sandpaper letters the child learns to recognize the letters by sight and touch, as well as by hearing each letter spoken. He feels the letters with his fingers, tracing their outline in the same direction in which he will eventually write them.

The child learns while his hand works, and he must handle the letters and become familiar with them before either reading or writing is possible. Through the movable alphabet he acquires a familiarity with the alphabet and sees how letters are put together to form words.

The alphabet sounds are learned individually, then combined to form short words. The child sounds these words out phonetically—slowly at first, stressing each sound. Gradually he is able to blend the individual sounds together and say the whole word.

For the four-year-old, reading and writing are a fascinating game, and he is eager to learn and master these skills. Through repeated work with the materials, the child's reading and writing skills are developed and perfected, and gradually new and more advanced lessons are introduced.

Language development too is an integral part of the process of learning to read and write. The importance of good speech cannot be overstressed because it is the means by which the child makes himself known and understood. It gives the child a feeling of equality with his peers, as well as facilitating future learning.

In helping to build your child's vocabulary, remember these few basic steps:

1) Speak distinctly to the child—avoid baby talk.
2) Teach correct names of people and objects.
3) Read to your child.
4) Give him good books to look at—remember that pictures stimulate the imagination and lead to conversation.
5) Talk to him.
6) Listen to him when he talks to you.
7) Let him listen to records.
8) Encourage his talking with other children and adults.
9) In working with various materials, compare and contrast (large–small, large–larger–largest, etc.).
10) Use the three-period lesson.

SANDPAPER LETTERS
AGE 3–5

MATERIALS: Mounted sandpaper letters, either upper or lower case (See instructions for making sandpaper numbers and letters on pages following page 97)

DEMONSTRATION:
1) Take two letters of contrasting shape and sound to the child's table.
2) With the child's two "working fingers" (index and second fingers) trace the letter and tell him the letter sound.
3) Use the three-period lesson with each letter.
4) Explain to the child that words are composed of these letters.
5) If you have used, for example, the *b* and *s* you can say "Can you hear *b* when I say 'belt'?" "Can you think of words with a *b* sound in them?" Do the same with the *s*.
6) Give the child more letters as he becomes ready for them, always using two letters at a time and using the procedure described above.

PURPOSE: To learn to recognize the forms and letters of the alphabet by touch, sight and hearing; to get the "feel" of the letters as a preparation for writing

NOTE: Be sure that the child traces the letters in the same direction as he would normally write them. Follow the alphabet chart. Upper or lower case may be used first. Teach the *sound,* not the name of the letter.

Familiarity with the alphabet is necessary before the child can read or write. Merely looking at the letters is not enough—the child must handle the letters and actually "feel" them.

The Correct Way to Write Letters

Aa Bb Cc Dd Ee

Ff Gg Hh Ii Jj Kk

Ll Mm Nn Oo Pp

Qq Rr Ss Tt Uu

Vv Ww Xx Yy Zz

COMMAND CARDS
AGE 3–5

MATERIALS:
Cards (Instructions for making command cards on page 92)

DEMONSTRATION:
1) First introduce the one-word command cards, one at a time. Point to the command and tell the child what it says.
2) Let the child act out what it says.
3) As the child comes to recognize each command it becomes necessary only to hold a particular card up silently, and let him obey.
4) As the one-word commands become easy for the child, gradually introduce the sentence commands in the same way.

PURPOSE:
To associate the written word with the action
To prepare for reading

PICTURES AND SOUNDS
AGE 3½–5

MATERIALS: Sandpaper letters
Index box of pictures

DEMONSTRATION:

1) Pick the sound or sounds to be worked with. (Never use more than two sounds at a time.)

2) Let the child feel a letter with his fingers, saying the sound, then go to the index box and pick the pictures that go with that sound.

3) Each time a new picture is taken out, tell him to feel the letter again, to say the sound and then give the

name of the object in the picture. For example, the *b* sound would go with "ball," "boat," "bug," "boy."

4) Repeat the exercise throughout the alphabet.

PURPOSE: To familiarize the child with the alphabet sounds as used in words, and to enlarge his vocabulary

NOTE: Use the true sound of each letter first (e.g., *a* as in "apple"), then use the other sounds. Introduce combinations such as *ch* and *sh* last. Teach *x* as it is used at the end or in the middle of the word (e.g., "ax," "fox"), and pronounce it just as it sounds—"eks."

THE MOVABLE ALPHABET
AGE 4–5

MATERIALS:

Movable alphabet letters (Instructions for making movable alphabet on page 96)

DEMONSTRATION:

1) Give the child the box of letters and various picture cards with the name of the object written underneath —or use individual puzzle pieces with the name written on its corresponding space.

2) Let him spell each word out with the letters.

3) Next, give him a list of familiar words (e.g., sister, chair, cat) and let him proceed in the same way.

4) Show the box of letters to the child and ask him to select various letters for you. When he is able to do this with ease, choose simple three-letter words and ask, "What letters do you hear when I say 'cat'?" As he says each letter, ask him to pick that letter from the box and place it in front of him. Continue to make words with the child in this way, until he fully understands and is able to work by himself.

5) As he becomes more adept, give him a small box containing cutout pictures of objects with three-letter names. Let him place each object, one by one, on the table and with the letters write its name beside it.

PURPOSE: To learn to analyze and form words as a preparation for reading, writing and spelling

Part V
Arithmetic Exercises

Arithmetic Development

Sensorial training is of great importance in learning the basics of arithmetic. Montessori has a wide variety of materials for this purpose, thus allowing the child to become familiar with numbers at an early age when he is most responsive to this type of experience. The child of three has a very logical mind and is interested in sequence and order in his daily life. This follows through into his subsequent learning of arithmetic, enabling him to learn easily and enthusiastically. The idea of quantity is inherent in all the Montessori arithmetic materials and the conception of identity and difference in the sensorial exercises is built up from recognition of identical objects and gradation of similar objects.

The fundamental feature of our number system is the decimal system. Because we count in tens, all the early sensorial materials are limited to sets of tens, until the child has a thorough knowledge of the units.

The earliest sensorial introduction to arithmetic comes with the pink tower, which consists of ten cubes of gradated size. The first direct introduction to quantity comes with the number rods. These ten rods are also gradated in size, with each unit represented by one segment. When these rods have been placed in order of gradation, we teach the child the actual number name "one," "two," "three," etc.

Next the sandpaper numbers are introduced, enabling the child to learn the number name and see how it is written. The numbers are traced with the fingers in the direction in which they will be written, enabling the child to see how they are formed. The child thus learns the figures through seeing them, being told the name and touching the numbers with his fingers.

The sandpaper numbers and the number rods are then used together, uniting the written name and the quantity. With the rods, each separate quantity is one unit. The quantities are fixed; the symbols are loose and must be placed in order.

The spindle box is the next step in learning the fundamentals of arithmetic, and with it comes the child's first introduction to zero. "Zero" is defined as nothing; yet it is an indicator of value, and when placed next to one it enables the child to count beyond nine. With the spindle box the figures are fixed and in order, and it is the quantities which are loose.

Now the child is ready to use the sandpaper numbers and counters as directed in the exercise. In this lesson both the quantities *and* the figures are loose, and both must be placed in orderly sequence.

The young child is enabled through repeated work with these materials to learn the names of the numbers before grasping the abstract conceptions. He learns by repetition and gradually builds up a strong basis for more advanced arithmetic.

NUMBER RODS
AGE 3–5

MATERIALS: Number rods (cut from patterns on page 111)

Small cards with numbers 1 to 10 written on them

DEMONSTRATION:

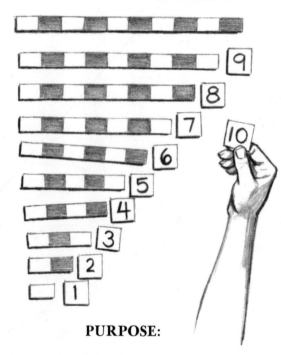

1) Place the No. 1 rod on the table, saying "one."
2) Place the No. 2 rod parallel to this and say "two"; then, pointing to each section, say "one," "two."
3) Proceed in much the same manner as with the counters and sandpaper numbers (showing by pointing to each section that "two is one more than 'one,'" etc.).
4) When the procedure is completed and all ten rods are out, place the corresponding numbers by each rod, explaining to the child what you are doing.

PURPOSE: To further familiarize the child with the numbers and the association of name with quantity

NOTE: When the numbers and their quantities are familiar to the child, use the number rods to teach addition. Show how $9 + 1 = 10$, $8 + 2 = 10$, $7 + 3 = 10$, etc. by placing the No. 1 rod next to the No. 9 rod, the No.

2 next to No. 8, etc. Proceed in this manner to show the child other addition combinations. Then, reversing the same method, teach subtraction.

THE SPINDLE BOX
AGE 3–5

MATERIAL: Spindle box (Instructions for making spindle box on page 95)

DEMONSTRATION:
1) Remove the spindles from all the compartments.
2) Beginning with the first compartment, say aloud the number written on the compartment and then put back the spindles while counting out the corresponding number.
3) Proceed in this manner with each compartment until all the spindles have been placed in the box.

PURPOSE: To teach association of numbers and quantities
To introduce zero

CONTROL OF ERROR: There are enough spindles to do the exercise correctly. If any spindles are left over, or if there are not enough to finish, it will be obvious to the child that he has made mistakes.

SANDPAPER NUMBERS
AGE 3–5

MATERIALS:

Sandpaper numbers (Instructions for making sandpaper numbers and letters on pages following page 97)

45 counters (chips, buttons, etc.)

DEMONSTRATION:

1) Show the child the first two joints in the first two fingers. Flex them and show how they work, explaining that these two fingers do all the work.

2) Begin with the zero, explaining that it means nothing, and tracing it with the two fingers.

3) Say the number "one," as you place it on the floor by the zero. Trace it and place one counter by it to show that one object is the same as the symbol for one. Show that one is one more than zero.

4) As each new number is introduced, repeat and count: 0, 1, 2, 3, 4. Use the three-period lesson.

5) Give value to the symbols by placing counters of corresponding value next to them. Show that three is one more than two, two is one more than one, etc.

6) Be sure that the child knows and understands the meaning of zero to four, then proceed with the numbers through nine in the same way. Repeat number value, add objects and return to zero for each number taught.

PURPOSE: To introduce the child to numbers and to teach him the association of the number name and the corresponding quantity

WRITING NUMBERS
AGE 4–5

MATERIALS: A small blackboard or sheet of paper, divided into squares

DEMONSTRATION:
1) In the first vertical row of squares, to the far left of the paper, write the numbers 1 to 9.
2) Let the child copy these numbers in the squares following each number.
3) This can also be done with alphabet letters.

PURPOSE: To teach the child the fundamentals of writing

NOTE: The exercise may be done another way. Let the child clip a piece of tracing paper over a sheet on which the numbers or letters have been written, and trace them with a pencil, always being sure to move his pencil in the correct "writing" direction.

The Correct Way to Write Numbers

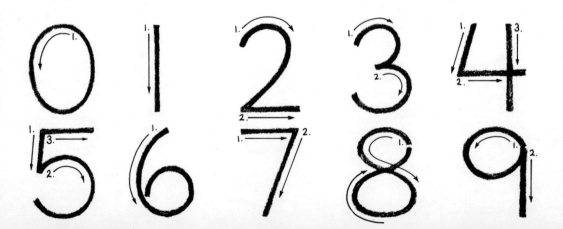

NUMBER PROGRESSION
AGE 4½–5

MATERIALS: The numbers 1 to 100 (cut from patterns on page 98)

DEMONSTRATION:

1) Present the numbers to the child in proper sequence, one at a time, and ask him to line them up on the floor. (Use the chart on the following pages for proper sequence.)

2) Have the child say each number aloud as he does this.

3) When all the numbers are out, show the child 0 through 9, as he is most familiar with these numbers.

4) Show him how the next line has the figure *1* in front of each of these numbers; the following line will have the number *2,* and so on through the sequence.

5) When the child is thoroughly familiar with his numbers, explain the odd and even numbers to him. Write out the chart, coloring the even numbers red, and the odd numbers blue.

PURPOSE: To allow the child to build up the sequence of numbers and to have a visual impression of odd and even numbers

To prepare the child for mathematics

Number Progression Chart

0	1	2	3	4	5	6	7	8	9
10	11	12	13	14	15	16	17	18	19
20	21	22	23	24	25	26	27	28	29
30	31	32	33	34	35	36	37	38	39
40	41	42	43	44	45	46	47	48	49

50	51	52	53	54	55	56	57	58	59
60	61	62	63	64	65	66	67	68	69
70	71	72	73	74	75	76	77	78	79
80	81	82	83	84	85	86	87	88	89
90	91	92	93	94	95	96	97	98	99
100									

MEASURING EXERCISES
AGE 4–5

MATERIALS: Clear plastic 1-cup measurer
Plastic measurers of ½, ¼ and ⅓ cups
Measuring spoons
Cup of beans or rice

DEMONSTRATION:
1) At first let the child experiment with these things by himself by filling the cups with rice or beans from individual spoons or cups.
2) When the child appears ready, show him how many ¼ cups go into a cup, how many tablespoons go into ½ cup, etc.
3) Teach the child slowly and carefully, always explaining carefully what you are doing.

PURPOSE: To teach coordination of eye and hand
To introduce fractions

Part VI
Home Montessori Equipment
How to Make Your Equipment

PAINT AND PLAY DOUGH

FINGERPAINT:

Mix together:
1 cup laundry starch
1 cup cold water
3 cups soap flakes
Add a small drop of food coloring or powdered paint for color.

CLAY (play dough):

3 cups flour
1 cup salt
1 cup water (with coloring)
1 tablespoon oil
Mix the flour and salt, add water and oil gradually, mixing until proper consistency is reached. This can be kept in the refrigerator when not in use.

EASEL PAINT: Use powdered tempera, slowly adding water until the proper consistency is reached. It is best to make a small amount at a time and to avoid a too liquid consistency. Small tin cans are excellent for mixing the paints, and the child can paint directly from them. Be sure to show the child how to remove the excess paint from the brush to avoid an unnecessary mess.

BUSY BOARD

WHAT YOU WILL NEED: A board approximately 12″ x 18″

Upholstery tacks

Pieces of fabric with a hook, snap, button, zipper, shoelace, buckle, safety pin and two pieces of twill tape or ribbon for tying a bow

HOW TO MAKE: Attach each object to the board with tacks, being sure to leave enough flexibility in the material to allow the child to work easily.

Remember to use a board of a size that would enable the child to reach all parts of it with ease.

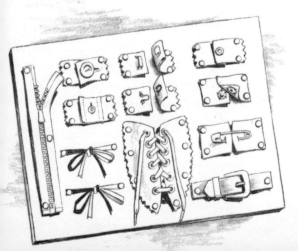

INDIVIDUAL DRESSING FRAMES

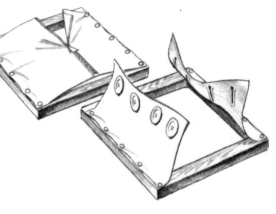

WHAT YOU WILL NEED:	Eight frames of wood approximately 10″ square
	Upholstery tacks
	Enough fabric for each frame
	One jacket-type zipper
	4 large buttons
	4 snaps
	4 hooks
	shoelace
	4 buckles
	4 large safety pins
	4 red pieces of twill tape or ribbon, approximately 12″ long
	4 white pieces of twill tape or ribbon, approximately 12″ long
HOW TO MAKE:	Make a separate dressing frame, using each of the above items, as shown in the illustration.
NOTE:	A large doll may be used instead. Dress her in clothes utilizing snaps, buttons, etc.
	Use the cloth books *All by Himself* or *All by Herself*.

BARIC TABLETS

WHAT YOU WILL NEED:	5–6 pieces of board of gradually differing weights and measuring approximately 3″ x 4″
SUGGESTION:	Begin with lightest-weight balsa and work up to plywood. The pieces may be painted if you wish.

COMMAND CARDS

WHAT YOU WILL NEED:

18–20 cards, approximately 8½" x 3"
A broad-tipped pen or crayon

HOW TO MAKE:

On each individual card, in lower-case letters, print the following commands: walk, run, sit, stand, jump, hop, skip, talk, tap, sing; come here, sit down, be quiet, stand up, lie down, bring me the book, pick up the pencil, close the door, open the door, etc.

ROUGH AND SMOOTH BOARDS

WHAT YOU WILL NEED:

Three wooden rectangular boards (approximately 4" x 8")
Sandpaper of five gradated textures
Scissors
Glue (contact or cement)

HOW TO MAKE:

Board I: Glue smooth sandpaper on one half of the board and rough sandpaper on the other half.

Board II: Glue on the board 1" alternate strips of smooth and rough sandpaper.

Board III: Glue on the board five strips of differently textured sandpaper, ranging from very smooth to very rough.

SCENT BOTTLES

WHAT YOU WILL NEED:
Twelve plastic or glass bottles of the same size

One sheet of colored paper or contact paper

Six spices (e.g., clove, tea, cinnamon, nutmeg, bay leaf)

HOW TO MAKE:
Cut paper to wrap around the outside of each bottle.

Put red tops on half of the bottles, and blue tops on the other half.

Fill two bottles each (one red top, one blue top) with the same spice.

Keep these in a small shoe box or other container.

OR:
Use flip-top cigarette boxes, plastic pill vials, spice bottles, or plastic salt and pepper shakers.

Soak a cotton ball in liquid flavorings and place each one in a separate covered bottle.

SOUND BOTTLES

WHAT YOU WILL NEED:
Twelve plastic bottles of the same size

Colored paper or contact paper

Six "sounds" (e.g., beans, whole pepper, rice, tea, sugar, salt)

HOW TO MAKE:
Make in the same manner as the scent bottles.

THERMAL BOTTLES

WHAT YOU WILL NEED: 6 small plastic or glass containers

HOW TO MAKE: Fill each container with water of varying temperatures ranging from very cold to very hot.

NOTE: For obvious reasons this exercise must be done as soon as the containers are prepared.

COLOR TABLETS

WHAT YOU WILL NEED: 60–80 2″ x 3″ pieces of lightweight balsa
Paint (all colors)

HOW TO MAKE: BOX I: Paint three pairs of board in the primary colors (red, blue, yellow).

BOX II: Paint eleven pairs of board in the following colors: red, blue, yellow, orange, green, purple, pink, gray, brown, black, white.

BOX III: Paint boards in six to eight shades of the following: red, blue, yellow, green, orange, purple, gray, brown.

OR: Use spools of thread coated with clear nail polish to prevent unraveling.

OR: Get color sample cards from your local paint dealer and mount them individually on heavy cardboard.

COLOR CIRCLES

WHAT YOU WILL NEED:

Paper in six to eight different colors
Scissors
Glue
String

HOW TO MAKE:

Cut a circle from each sheet of paper.

On each, paste a white strip with the color name printed in either upper or lower case.

Punch a hole at the top of each circle and join them together loosely with string (in tablet fashion).

SPINDLE BOX

WHAT YOU WILL NEED:

45 spindles (dowels, popsicle sticks, plastic spoons, etc.)

A box large enough to be divided into ten compartments into which your chosen spindles can be fitted.

HOW TO MAKE:

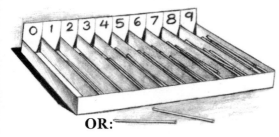

1) Divide your box into ten equal compartments.
2) Number the compartments 0 to 9.
3) Place the correct number of spindles in each compartment.

OR:

Use a muffin tin, with each cup numbered, and use buttons or beads for counters.

PICTURES AND SOUNDS

WHAT YOU WILL NEED:
Recipe box
Index dividers A to Z
1–2 packages plain index cards
Old magazines, greeting cards, catalogs, etc.
Glue

HOW TO MAKE:
1) Go through old magazines, etc., and cut out 6 to 8 pictures for each alphabet letter. For example, for *i* you could use inch, ice, iron, insect, igloo, ink; for *y* yo-yo, yard, yarn, yolk, yam; and for *z* zebra, zero, zoo, zucchini.
2) Paste each picture on an index card and file in the box behind its corresponding sound.

NOTE:
You will discover that it is easy to find numerous pictures for some letters and very difficult to find them for others.

MOVABLE ALPHABET

WHAT YOU WILL NEED:
Cardboard
Scissors
Heavy pencil or crayon

HOW TO MAKE:
1) Draw 312 1″ x 1″ squares.
2) Write six upper-case and six

lower-case letters for each letter of the alphabet.

3) Cut into squares.

OR: Purchase plastic, wood, felt or cardboard letters.

NOTE: For convenience and easy use, keep the pieces in a box with divisions for each letter. This enables the child to find the letters easily. To save space, both the upper- and lower-case of each letter may be kept in one division. Plastic divider boxes used for fishing tackle are excellent for this purpose.

SANDPAPER NUMBERS AND LETTERS

WHAT YOU WILL NEED:
12 sheets of black emery paper
enough white poster board for 58 6″ x 6″ squares
Sharp scissors
Glue (contact or cement)

HOW TO MAKE:
From poster-board cut 58 6″ x 6″ squares.

Using patterns on following pages, cut numbers and letters from emery paper. Glue each letter or number to a square.

1234
567
890

76571

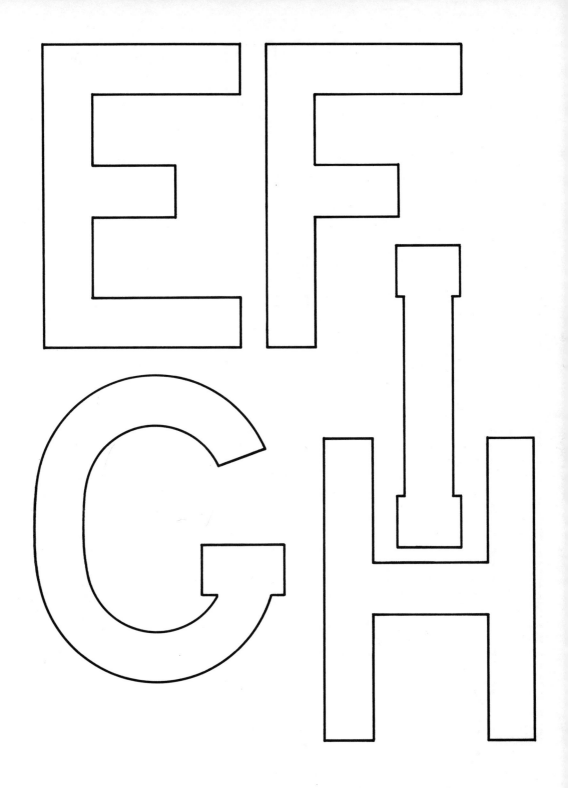

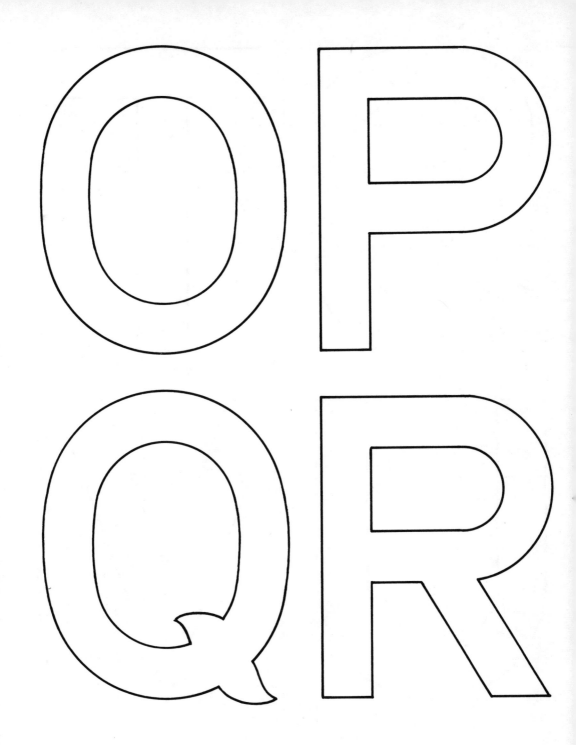

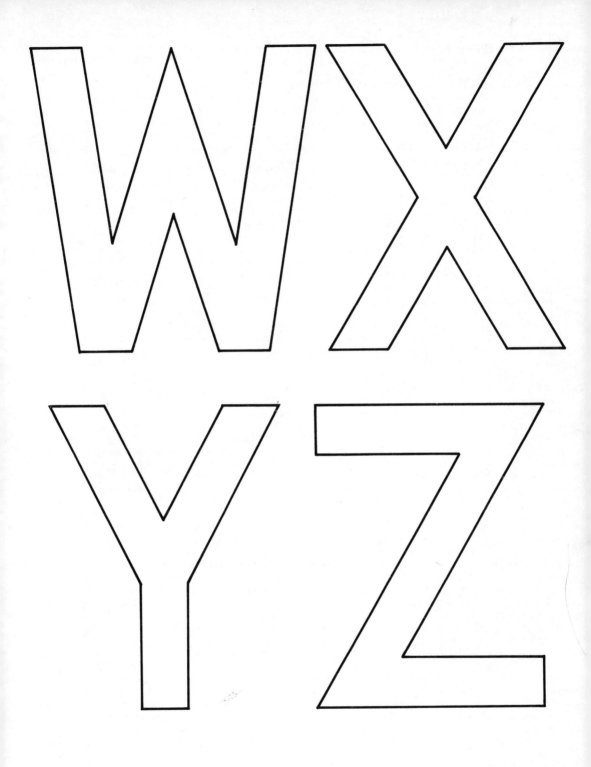

GEOMETRIC INSETS

WHAT YOU WILL NEED:

2 contrasting colors of heavy poster board (red and blue)
6 gold brads
Scissors
Ruler

HOW TO MAKE:

Cut six 5" x 5" squares from the red board.

Using the patterns, cut the insets from the middle and discard.

Using the patterns, cut the geometric insets from the blue board, attach a gold brad (used as a knob for the child to grasp) to the center of each.

Place the blue insets inside their corresponding red frames. Place the six frames and insets on a standard-size cookie sheet (three on top row, three on bottom) for convenience and to enable the child to see them all together.

NUMBER RODS AND NUMBERS

WHAT YOU WILL NEED:

Poster board or balsa
Glue
Scissors
Red and blue pencils or paint

HOW TO MAKE:

Using the patterns, cut rods from balsa or poster board or simply cut the individual pattern rods and glue them to a heavy poster board. Color the No. 1 rod red, the No. 2 rod red, blue, No. 3 rod red, blue, red, etc. Each unit is represented by a 1″ segment of alternate color.

Cut the individual numbers from the pattern and glue each on a piece of poster board of corresponding size.

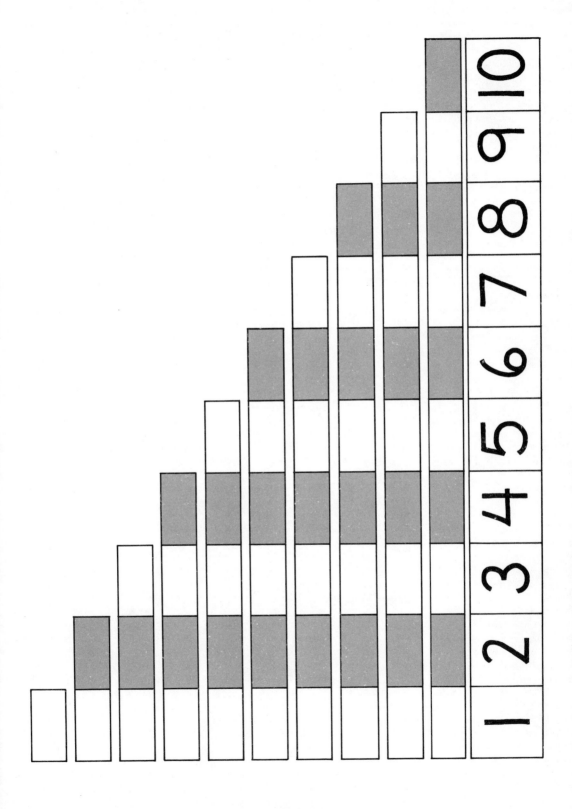

Appendix

MONTESSORI TERMS

Absorbent mind The ability and ease with which the young child learns unconsciously from his environment.

Control of error The possibility inherent in the Montessori materials of making apparent the mistakes made by the child, thereby allowing him to see his errors after completing the exercises and to correct them.

Cycles of activity Those periods of concentration on a particular task that should be worked to completion.

Deviated child The child who has not yet found himself and thus is restless and difficult to control. He finds adjustment difficult and often escapes into a fantasy world.

Didactic materials The instructive materials used in teaching.

Discovery of the child Dr. Montessori's awareness and realization of the young child's abilities and his spontaneous love of work and learning.

Freedom The child's free movements and experiences in an environment that provides discipline through liberty and respect for his rights.

Normalized child The child who adapts easily and has acquired the self-discipline and control necessary to a healthy life.

Practical life exercises Those exercises through which the child learns to care for himself and his environment.

Prepared environment   An atmosphere created to enable the child to be free to learn through activity in peaceful and orderly surroundings adapted to the child's size and interests.

Sensitive periods   Those periods of learning (to walk, talk, write, etc.) during which a child is particularly sensitive to a specific stimulus.

Sensorial exercises   Those exercises pertaining to the development of the five senses and for providing a foundation for speech, writing and arithmetic by use of the sensorial materials.

Sensorial materials   The Montessori equipment designed to teach the child by means of focusing the mind on specific sensory responses.

EDUCATIONAL TOYS

When choosing toys for your child, try to pick things that will challenge him as well as stimulate his own creativity and imagination. The toys that make use of the hand and mind at the same time are excellent. Two or three educational-toy catalogs are a must in every home with children—they not only have a marvelous selection of things that may be purchased but they can also give you ideas for making things at home.

Excellent catalogs (which include Montessori materials) may be obtained by writing to any of the following:

> Childcraft Equipment Co.
> P. O. Box 280
> Madison Square Station
> New York, N. Y. 10010
>
> Creative Playthings
> 5757 West Century Blvd.
> Los Angeles, Calif. 90045
>
> *or*
>
> Creative Playthings
> Princeton, N. J.
>
> Lakeshore Equipment Co.
> 1144 Montague Avenue
> San Leandro, Calif. 94577
>
> Teaching Aids (Montessori equipment)
> Division of A. Daigger & Co.
> 159 West Kinzie St.
> Chicago, Ill.
>
> St. Nicholas' Training Centre (Montessori equipment)
> 15 Dawson Place
> London W. 2, England

The following is a partial list of useful materials and their brand names. This is meant to give you a better idea of what type of thing to look for in stores and catalogs. Discount stores and trading-stamp redemption centers are also good places to shop; they usually carry top brand names.

Development of Early Motor Skills and Sensory Perception

Parquetry Blocks	Playskool
Lacing Boot	Playskool
Jumbo Beads	Playskool
Inside U. S. Map Puzzle	Playskool
Postal Station	Playskool
Col-o-Rol Wagon	Playskool
Lincoln Logs	Playskool
Match Picture—Match Word Games	Playskool
Puzzles by Sifo and Simplex	Creative Playthings
Go-Together Cards	Creative Playthings
Color Cone	Creative Playthings
Perception Plaques	Creative Playthings
Kitten in Kegs	Child Guidance
Learning Tower	Child Guidance
Tinker Toys	The Toy Tinkers
Play Tiles	Halsam
Fit-a-Shape	Lauri Enterprises
Alph-a-Space	Lauri Enterprises
Etch-a-Sketch	Ohio Art
Stick-on-Games	Colorforms
Play with Felt	Milton Bradley
Puzzles	Whitman
Easy Sticker Fun	Whitman
Color Books	Whitman
Stencil and Snip	Whitman
Follow the Dot Books	Whitman

Miscellaneous Items

sewing cards	lotto games	blackboard	magnetic board
magic slates	cutting games	rhyming games	tracing shapes
paper dolls	perception and discrimination games		records

Language Development and Aids to Reading and Writing

Capital and Lower-Case Letters	Creative Playthings
Magnetic Spelling Board	Teach-a-Tot
Quizmo	Milton Bradley

Word Builder	Milton Bradley
Cardboard Letters	Milton Bradley
Link Letters	Milton Bradley
Play With Felt (letters and shapes)	Milton Bradley
Rhyming Words	Ideal School Supply

Miscellaneous Items

books   records   blackboard

Arithmetic

Clock Face with Movable Gears	Creative Playthings
Giant-Grooved Domino Blocks	Creative Playthings
Number Sorter	Creative Playthings
Teach a Time Clock	Child Guidance
Learning Numbers	Child Guidance
Add a Count Scale	Child Guidance
Roundup	Industrial Plastics
Follow the Number Books	Whitman
Cardboard Numbers	Milton Bradley
Bingo	Milton Bradley
Day-by-Day Calender	Milton Bradley

BIBLIOGRAPHY

Fisher, Dorothy Canfield, Montessori for Parents, *rev. ed. Cambridge, Massachusetts, Robert Bentley Incorporated, 1965.*

Fisher, Dorothy Canfield, The Montessori Manual for Teachers and Parents, *rev. ed. Cambridge, Massachusetts, Robert Bentley Incorporated, 1964.*

Montessori, Maria, The Absorbent Mind. *Wheaton, Illinois, The Theosophical Publishing House, 1963.*

Montessori, Maria, Dr. Montessori's Own Handbook. *New York, Schocken Books, 1965.*

Montessori, Maria, The Montessori Method. *Cambridge, Massachusetts, Robert Bentley, Incorporated, 1965.*

Montessori, Maria, The Formation of Man. *Adyar, India, The Theosophical Publishing House, 1962.*

Montessori, Maria, What You Should Know about Your Child. *Adyar, India, Kalakshetra Publications, 1961.*

Montessori, Maria, The Child. *Adyar, India, The Theosophical Publishing House, 1948.*

Montessori, Maria, The Discovery of the Child. *Adyar, India, Kalakshetra Publications, 1948.*

Montessori, Maria, Education for a New World. *Adyar, India, Kalakshetra Publications, 1946.*

Montessori, Maria, Peace and Education. *Geneva, International Bureau of Education, 1932.*

Montessori, Maria, The Secret of Childhood. *London, Longmans, Green and Company, 1936.*

Montessori, Maria, Reconstruction in Education. *Adyar, India, Theosophical Publishing House, 1948.*

Montessori, Maria, Pedagogical Anthropology. *New York, Frederick A. Stokes Company, 1913.*

Montessori, Maria, Dr. Montessori's Own Handbook. *Cambridge, Massachusetts, Robert Bentley, Incorporated, 1965.*

Montessori, Maria, The Montessori Method. *Cambridge, Massachusetts, Robert Bentley, Incorporated, 1965.*

Montessori, Maria, Spontaneous Activity in Education. *Cambridge, Massachusetts, Robert Bentley, Incorporated, 1965.*

Montessori, Maria, The Montessori Elementary Material. *Cambridge, Massachusetts, Robert Bentley, Incorporated, 1965.*

Montessori, Maria, To Educate the Human Potential. *Adyar, India, Kalakshetra Publications, 1948.*

Montessori, Mario, Dr. Montessori and Her Work. *London, W. Knott & Son.*

Orem, R. C., A Montessori Handbook. *New York, G. P. Putnam's Sons, 1965.*

Rambusch, Nancy McCormick, Learning How to Learn. *Baltimore, Maryland, Helicon Press, 1962.*

St. Nicholas' Training Centre for the Montessori Method of Education, Correspondence Course for the Nursery Diploma

Standing, E. M., Maria Montessori: Her Life and Work. *Fresno, California, Academy Guild Press, 1959.*

Standing, E. M., The Montessori Revolution in Education, *New York, Schocken Books, 1966.*

Stevens, Ellen Yale, A Guide to the Montessori Method. *New York, Frederick A. Stokes Company, 1913.*

Ward, Florence Elizabeth, The Montessori Method and the American School. *New York, The Macmillan Company, 1913.*

About the Author

ELIZABETH G. HAINSTOCK became interested in the Montessori method during its recent revival in the United States. She received her Montessori certification from St. Nicholas' Training Centre, London, and began working at home with her preschool children. She worked with the College of Notre Dame at Belmont, California, in bringing the Montessori system into the home, by lecturing to parents and teachers about her personal program and its success. Mrs. Hainstock lectures extensively and conducts classes for parents and teachers. She lives in Palo Alto, California, with her husband and three daughters.